This journal belongs to

_____

Faith

© 2011 Ellie Claire Gift and Paper Corp.

www.ellieclaire.com

Designed by Lisa and Jeff Franke

ISBN 978-1-60936-236-2

Printed in China

FAITH

*A new path lies before us; we're not sure where it leads;
But God goes on before us, providing all our needs.*

Linda Maurice

Your ears shall hear a word behind you, saying,
"This is the way, walk in it," whenever you turn to the
right hand or whenever you turn to the left.

Isaiah 30:21 NKJV

*Never be afraid to trust an unknown future
to an all-knowing God.*

Corrie ten Boom

reat is the Lord and greatly to be praised; and His greatness is unsearchable.... The Lord is good to all, and His tender mercies are over all His works.

Psalm 145:3, 9 NIV

Love is there for us, love so great that it does not turn its face away from us. That Love is Jesus. We can dare to hope and believe again.

Gloria Gaither

Now faith, hope, and love abide, these three;
and the greatest of these is love.

1 Corinthians 13:13 NRSV

I see Heaven's glories shine, and faith shines equal, arming me from fear.

Emily Brontë

O Lord, our Lord, how excellent is Your name in all
the earth, who have set Your glory above the heavens.

Psalm 8:1 NKJV

*You are a child of your heavenly Father. Confide in Him.
Your faith in His love and power can never be bold enough.*

Basilea Schlink

When I called, You answered me;
You made me bold and stouthearted.

Psalm 138:3 NIV

The hope we have is a living hope, an unassailable one. We wait for it, in faith and patience.

Elisabeth Elliot

Yet those who wait for the Lord will gain new strength; they will mount up with wings like eagles, they will run and not get tired, they will walk and not become weary.

Isaiah 40:31 NASB

The most effective, distinctly Christian way
to show our love for God is to trust Him.

Eugenia Price

Our help is in the name of the Lord,
who made heaven and earth.

Psalm 124:8 NRSV

God doesn't want us to just depend on Him as a last resort....
He wants us to depend on Him for every breath we take.
And...that kind of dependent life is not stifling. It's liberating!

Stormie Omartian

We have come to know and have believed the love which God has for us. God is love, and the one who abides in love abides in God, and God abides in him.

1 John 4:16 NASB

When I need a dose of wonder I wait for a clear night and go look for the stars.... Often the wonder of the stars is enough to return me to God's loving grace.

Madeleine L'Engle

And now I entrust you to God and the message of His
grace that is able to build you up and give you an
inheritance with all those He has set apart for Himself.

Acts 20:32 NLT

Lord...give me the gift of faith.... Teach me to live this moment only, looking neither to the past with regret, nor the future with apprehension. Let love be my aim and my life a prayer.

Roseann Alexander-Isham

Since we have so great a cloud of witnesses surrounding us, let us...lay aside every encumbrance...and let us run with endurance the race that is set before us.

Hebrews 12:1 NASB

God has not called me to be successful;
He has called me to be faithful.

Mother Teresa

the Lord search the mind and try the heart, to give to every man according to his ways, according to the fruit of his doings.

Jeremiah 17:10 NRSV

No journey carries one far unless, as it extends into the world around us, it goes an equal distance into the world within.

Lillian Smith

The fear of the Lord is the beginning of wisdom;
all who follow His precepts have good understanding.

Psalm 111:10 NIV

I believe that life is given us so we may grow in love.
Helen Keller

_____

_____

_____

_____

_____

_____

_____

_____

_____

_____

_____

_____

_____

_____

_____

_____

We ought always to thank God for you...and rightly so, because your faith is growing more and more, and the love every one of you has for each other is increasing.

2 Thessalonians 1:3 NIV

Faith is not believing that God can—
it's knowing that He will.

*B*ehold, I am with you and will keep you wherever you go, and will bring you back to this land; for I will not leave you until I have done what I have promised you.

Genesis 28 : 15 NASB

Faith expects from God what is beyond all expectations.

Those who trust God's action in them find that God's Spirit is in them—living and breathing God!

Romans 8:5 THE MESSAGE

Our feelings do not affect God's facts. They may blow up, like clouds, and cover the eternal things that we do most truly believe. We may not see the shining of the promises—but they still shine!

Amy Carmichael

To keep a firm grip on the faith.... It won't be long before this generous God who has great plans for us in Christ... will have you put together and on your feet for good.

1 Peter 5:9-10 THE MESSAGE

The soft, sweet summer was warm and glowing,
bright were the blossoms on every bough: I trusted Him
when the roses were blooming; I trust Him now.

S. B. Bowman

Know that wisdom is such to your soul; if you find it,
you will find a future, and your hope will not be cut off.

Proverbs 24:14 NRSV

If we just give God the little that we have,
we can trust Him to make it go around.
Gloria Gaither

Pure gold put in the fire comes out of it proved pure; genuine faith put through this suffering comes out proved genuine.... It's your faith, not your gold, that God will have on display as evidence of His victory.

1 Peter 1:6-7 THE MESSAGE

You have to have faith that there is a reason you go through certain things. I can't say I am glad to go through pain, but in a way one must, in order to gain courage and really feel joy.

Carol Burnett

"No one who trusts God like this—heart and soul—will ever regret it." It's exactly the same no matter what.... The same God for all of us, acting the same incredibly generous way.

Romans 10:11-12 THE MESSAGE

I took an inventory and looked into my little bag to see what I had left over. I had one jewel left in the bag, the brightest jewel of all. I had the gift of faith.

Lola Falana

God will do this, for He is faithful to do what He says, and He has invited you into partnership with His Son, Jesus Christ our Lord.

1 Corinthians 1:9 NLT

Fear not tomorrow, God is already there.

And I am convinced that nothing can ever separate us from God's love. Neither death nor life, neither angels nor demons, neither our fears for today nor our worries about tomorrow.

Romans 8:38 NLT

I never spoke with God nor visited in Heaven,
Yet certain am I of the spot as if the chart were given.

Emily Dickinson

The heavens proclaim His righteousness,
and all the peoples behold His glory.

Psalm 97:6 NRSV

It is a law of the spiritual life that every act of trust makes the next act less difficult.

Hannah Whitall Smith

As for God, His way is perfect; the word of the Lord
is proven; He is a shield to all who trust in Him.

2 Samuel 22:31 NKJV

Faith allows us to continually delight in life since we have placed our needs in God's hands.

Janet L. Weaver Smith

will answer them before they even call to Me. While they are still talking about their needs, I will go ahead and answer their prayers!

Isaiah 65:24 NLT

Live fully each moment of today. Trust God to let you work through it. He will give you all you need. Don't skip over the painful...moment—even it has its important and rightful place.

Go after God, who piles on all the riches
we could ever manage.

1 Timothy 6:17 THE MESSAGE

They that trust the Lord find many things to praise Him for. Praise follows trust.

Lily May Gould

And they sang responsively, praising and giving thanks to
the Lord: "For He is good, for His mercy endures forever."

Ezra 3:11 NKJV

I pray hard, work hard, and leave the rest to God.
Florence Griffith Joyner

Those who know Your name will put their trust in You,
for You, O Lord, have not forsaken those who seek You.

Psalm 9:10 NASB

God does many things which we do not understand....
A true faith must rest solidly on [God's] character and His Word,
not on our particular conceptions of what He ought to do.

Elisabeth Elliot

Faith is the assurance of things hoped for,
the conviction of things not seen.

Hebrews 11:1 NRSV

If you are at a place in your life where you feel like you can't take one step without the Lord's help, be glad. He has you where He wants you.

Stormie Omartian

Remember now, O Lord,...how I have walked
before You in faithfulness and with a whole heart,
and have done what is good in Your sight.

Isaiah 38:3 NRSV

Turn your eyes upon Jesus, look full in His wonderful face, and the things of earth will grow strangely dim, by the light of His glory and grace.

Helen Timmel

Let us fix our eyes on Jesus, the author and perfecter of our faith, who for the joy set before Him endured the cross, ...and sat down at the right hand of the throne of God.

Hebrews 12:2 NIV

Faith is the subtle chain that binds us to the infinite.
Elizabeth Oakes Smith

The Lord's loving kindnesses indeed never cease,
for His compassions never fail. They are new
every morning; great is Your faithfulness.

Lamentations 3: 22-23 NASB

Great faith isn't the ability to believe long and far into the misty future. It's simply taking God at His word and taking the next step.

Joni Eareckson Tada

For the very structures of earth are God's; He has laid out His operations on a firm foundation. He protectively cares for His faithful friends, step by step.

1 Samuel 2:8-9 THE MESSAGE

If we really fully belong to God, then we must be at His disposal and we must trust in Him. We must never be preoccupied with the future. There is no reason to be. God is there.

Mother Teresa

Whom have I in heaven but You? And there
is nothing on earth that I desire other than You.

Psalm 73:25 NRSV

God is here. I have joyously discovered that He is always "up to something" in my life, and I am learning to quit second-guessing Him and simply trust the process.

Gloria Gaither

"*For* I know the plans that I have for you," declares the Lord, "plans for welfare and not for calamity to give you a future and a hope."

Jeremiah 29:11 NASB

To wait before the Lord. Wait in the stillness. And in that stillness, assurance will come to you. You will know that you are heard.

Amy Carmichael

The Lord longs to be gracious to you; He rises to
show you compassion. For the Lord is a God of justice.
Blessed are all who wait for Him!

Isaiah 30:18 NIV

Within each of us there is an inner place where the living God Himself longs to dwell, our sacred center of belief.

As you have received Christ Jesus the Lord, so walk in Him, having been firmly rooted and now being built up in Him and established in your faith.

Colossians 2:6-7 NASB

If God, like a father, denies us what we want now, it is in order to give us some far better thing later on. The will of God, we can rest assured, is invariably a better thing.

Elisabeth Elliot

God's kingdom isn't a matter of what you put in your stomach....
It's what God does with your life as He sets it right,
puts it together, and completes it with joy.

Romans 14:17 THE MESSAGE

Faith is what makes life bearable, with all its tragedies and ambiguities and sudden, startling joys.

Madeleine D'Engle

You have granted me life and loving kindness;
and Your care has preserved my spirit.

Job 10:12 NASB

Only those who see the invisible can do the impossible.

Your steadfast love, O Lord, extends to the heavens,
Your faithfulness to the clouds.

Psalm 36:5 NRSV

At the very heart and foundation of all God's dealings with us, however...mysterious they may be, we must dare to believe in and assert the infinite, unmerited, and unchanging love of God.

E. B. Towman

Therefore, since we have a great high priest who has gone through the heavens, Jesus the Son of God, let us hold firmly to the faith we profess.

Hebrews 4:14 NIV

To believe in something not yet proved and to underwrite it with our lives; it is the only way we can leave the future open.

Lillian Smith

You can no more show me your works apart from your faith than I can show you my faith apart from my works. Faith and works, works and faith, fit together hand in glove.

James 2:18 THE MESSAGE

God gives the very best to those
who leave the choice to Him.

"If you'll hold on to Me for dear life," says God, "...I'll give you the best of care if you'll only get to know and trust Me."

Psalm 91:14-16 THE MESSAGE

With God our trust can be...utterly free. In Him are no limitations, no flaws, no weaknesses. His judgment is perfect, His knowledge of us is perfect, His love is perfect. God alone is trustworthy.

Eugenia Price

ove God, your God. Walk in His ways. Keep His commandments, regulations, and rules so that you will live, really live, live exuberantly, blessed by God.

Deuteronomy 30:16 THE MESSAGE

O troubled heart, tho' thy foes unite, let thy faith be strong and thy armor bright; Thou shalt overcome thro' His pow'r and might, and more than conqu'ror be.

Fanny Crosby

In all these things we are more than conquerors
through Him who loved us.

Romans 8:37 NIV

Abandon yourself to His care and guidance, as a sheep in the care of a shepherd, and trust Him utterly.

Hannah Whitall Smith

On that day the Lord their God will rescue His people, just as a shepherd rescues his sheep. They will sparkle in His land like jewels in a crown.

Zechariah 9:16 NLT

One thing Jesus asks of me: that I lean upon Him;
that in Him alone I put complete trust; that I surrender
myself to Him unreservedly.

Mother Teresa

If you see that the job is too big for you, that it's something only God can do, and you trust Him to do it...that trusting-Him-to-do-it is what gets you set right with God, by God.

Romans 4:4 THE MESSAGE

Faith, the spiritual strong searchlight, illuminates the way, and although sinister doubts may lurk..., I walk unafraid toward the Enchanted Wood where...life and death are one in the Presence of the Lord.

Helen Keller

Even though I walk through the darkest valley, I fear no evil, for You are with me; Your rod and Your staff—they comfort me.

Psalm 23:4 NRSV

Faith does more than give reality to that which we do not see; it makes us look differently at visible things.

Joni Eareckson Tada

Now we see but a poor reflection as in a mirror; then we shall see face to face. Now I know in part; then I shall know fully, even as I am fully known.

1 Corinthians 13: 12 NIV

To build in darkness does require faith. But one day the light returns and you discover that you have become a fortress...; you may even find yourself...sought by others as a beacon in their dark.

Olga Rosmanith

Call upon Me in the day of trouble;
I shall rescue you, and you will honor Me.

Psalm 50:15 NASB

Not everyone possesses...a conspicuous talent. We are not equally blessed with great intellect or physical beauty or emotional strength. But we have all been given the same ability to be faithful.

Gigi Graham Tchividjian

Well done, my good and faithful servant. You have been faithful in handling this small amount, so now I will give you many more responsibilities. Let's celebrate together!

Matthew 25:21 NLT

Lord, grant me a quiet mind, that trusting Thee,
for Thou art kind, I may go on without a fear,
for Thou, my Lord, art always near.

Amy Carmichael

I will walk among you and be your God,
and you will be My people.

Leviticus 26:12 NIV

There is a difference between living *in* Christ and living *for* Christ.... He is more interested in the time you spend *with* Him than with the works you accomplish in His name.

Carolyn Dunn

Remain in Me, and I will remain in you.

John 15:4 NLT

The way may at times seem dark, but light will arise,
if you trust in the Lord, and wait patiently for Him.

Elizabeth T. King

*Day by day the Lord takes care of the innocent,
and they will receive an inheritance that lasts forever.*

Psalm 37:18 NLT

Finding acceptance with joy, whatever the circumstances of life—whether they are petty annoyances or fiery trials—this is a living faith that grows.

Mary Lou Steigleder

God blesses the people who patiently endure testing.
Afterward they will receive the crown of life that God
has promised to those who love Him.

James 1:12 NLT

Trust! The way will open, the right issue will come, the end will be peace, the cloud will be lifted, and the light of eternal noonday shall shine at last.

J. B. Dowman

There is hope in your future, says the Lord.

Jeremiah 31:17 NKJV

Faith is the bucket of power lowered by the rope of prayer into the well of God's abundance. What we bring up depends upon what we let down. We have every encouragement to use a big bucket.

Virginia Whitman

He shall be like a tree planted by the rivers of water, that brings forth its fruit in its season, whose leaf also shall not wither; and whatever he does shall prosper.

Psalm 1:3 NKJV

I know that God is faithful! I know that He answers prayers, many times in ways I may not understand.

Sheila Walsh

And the work of righteousness will be peace, and the
service of righteousness, quietness and confidence forever.

Isaiah 32:17 NASB

You can trust the Lord too little, but you can never trust Him too much.

My flesh and my heart fail; but God is the strength
of my heart and my portion forever.

Psalm 73:26 NKJV

Often God has to shut a door in our face, so that He can subsequently open the door through which He wants us to go.

Catherine Marshall

The Lord is just in all His ways and kind in all His doings.

Psalm 145:17 NRSV

When our days are filled with crying, we can trust that God, in time, will again bring laughter.

Janette Oke

For the joy of the Lord is your strength.
Nehemiah 8:10 NIV

When faithfulness is most difficult,
it can be most rewarding.

The Lord rewards everyone for his
righteousness and his faithfulness.

1 Samuel 26:23 NRSV

Father, help me to see the dark threads too as part of Your design. And so learn to trust You in all things.

Elizabeth Sherrill

Neither height nor depth, nor anything else in all creation,
will be able to separate us from the love of God
that is in Christ Jesus our Lord.

Romans 8:39 NIV

God makes a promise—faith believes it, hope anticipates it, patience quietly awaits it.

Lead me in Your truth and teach me, for You are the God
of my salvation; on You I wait all the day.

Psalm 25:5 NKJV

Faith...has sustained me—faith in the God of the Bible, a God, as someone once put it, not small enough to be understood but big enough to be worshipped.

Elisabeth Elliot

For the eyes of the Lord run to and fro throughout the whole earth, to show Himself strong on behalf of those whose heart is loyal to Him.

2 Chronicles 16:9 NKJV

I believe in the immortality of the soul because I have within me immortal longings.

Helen Keller

Jesus, our Savior. He broke the power of death and illuminated the way to life and immortality through the Good News.

2 Timothy 1:10 NLT

It is such a comfort to drop the tangles of life into God's hands and leave them there.

L. B. Cowman

And God is able to make all grace abound to you,
so that in all things at all times, having all that
you need, you will abound in every good work.

2 Corinthians 9:8 NIV

The soul should always stand ajar, ready to welcome the ecstatic experience.

Emily Dickinson

God rewrote the text of my life when I opened
the book of my heart to His eyes.

Psalm 18:24 THE MESSAGE

'Twant me, 'twas the Lord. I always told Him, "I trust You. I don't know where to go or what to do, but I expect You to lead me," and He always did.

Harriet Tubman

In Your unfailing love You will lead the people You have redeemed.
In Your strength You will guide them to Your holy dwelling.

Exodus 15:13 NIV

Faith is the ability to let your light shine even after your fuse is blown. Faith is seeing light with the eyes of your heart, when the eyes of your body see only darkness ahead.

Barbara Johnson

For Your steadfast love is higher than the heavens;
Your faithfulness reaches to the clouds.

Psalm 108:4 NRSV

God delights to meet the faith of one who looks up to Him and says, "Lord, You know that I cannot do this—but I believe that You can!"

Amy Carmichael

Be joyful in hope, patient in affliction, faithful in prayer.

Romans 12:12 NIV

Just as angels are attracted to the light of joy and kindness, so too are miracles attracted to the lamp of faith and love.

Mary Augustine

And the grace of our Lord was exceedingly abundant,
with faith and love which are in Christ Jesus.

1 Timothy 1:14 NKJV

When we trust, the Lord works. What is done
is not done by us, but by Him.
Hannah Whitall Smith

Lord, we show our trust in You by obeying Your laws;
our heart's desire is to glorify Your name.

Isaiah 26:8 NLT

Faith in small things has repercussions that ripple all the way out. In a huge, dark room a little match can light up the place.

Joni Eareckson Tada

If you have faith the size of a mustard seed, you will say to this mountain, "Move from here to there," and it will move, and nothing will be impossible for you.

Matthew 17:20 NRSV

We learn to believe by believing. We learn to love by loving.

Eugenia Price

Give thanks to God—He is good and His love never quits.

1 Chronicles 16:34 THE MESSAGE

Faith is the first factor in a life devoted to service. Without faith, nothing is possible. With it, nothing is impossible.

Mary McLeod Bethune

Know therefore that the Lord your God is God, the faithful God who maintains covenant loyalty with those who love Him and keep His commandments, to a thousand generations.

Deuteronomy 7:9 NRSV

*Confidence is not based on wishful thinking,
but in knowing that God is in control.*

Certainly God has heard; He has given
heed to the voice of my prayer.

Psalm 66:19 NASB

Trust is giving up what little I have in strength and power so I can confidently relax in His power and strength.
Gloria Gaither

No eye has seen, no ear has heard, and no mind has imagined what God has prepared for those who love Him.

1 Corinthians 2:9 NLT

Be faithful in little things, for in them our strength lies. To the good God nothing is little, because He is so great and we so small.

Mother Teresa

Everything in the heavens and on earth is Yours, O Lord....
Power and might are in Your hand, and at Your discretion
people are made great and given strength.

1 Chronicles 29:11–12 NLT

We have been greatly encouraged..., dear brothers and sisters, because you have remained strong in your faith.

1 Thessalonians 3:7 NLT